ME: I Can Make a Positive Difference!
Copyright © 2014 by Deborah A. Fotios

All rights reserved. Neither this publication nor any part of this publication may be reproduced or transmitted in any form or by any means, electronic or mechanical, including photocopying, recording or any information storage and retrieval system, without permission in writing from the author.

ISBN: 978-1-4866-0326-8

Word Alive Press
131 Cordite Road, Winnipeg, MB R3W 1S1
www.wordalivepress.ca

The late Honourable Jack Layton, Leader of the New Democratic Party of Canada.

"Love is better than anger. Hope is better than fear. Optimism is better than despair. So let us be loving, hopeful and optimistic. And we'll change the world."

Appreciations & Acknowledgments

Thanks be to Almighty God for His major contribution to this project (Rom 16:27, NLT).

To my parents, Fotios-Frank and Frieda-Theofano Kossyfas; my siblings, Bess and Jim-James. I love and appreciate you all.

My thanks and appreciation to Word Alive Press for the opportunity to publish a children's book.

To Whitby Montessori and Elementary School, in particular: Mrs. Cathy Barber, Principal and Pastor and Life Coach, Mr. Gary Francis, Ms. Jean of Faith Family Church, Ms. Vickie Scott, Consultant, Mr. & Mrs. Gray of Higher Marks, Pastor Femi Adegun of Teenagers' World and Pastor, Inspirational Author, Martins Fatola. Thank you to all.

Finally, to my beloved ministry team at Mountain of Fire & Miracles Ministries (MFM) Toronto-Markham, ON, CA. My sincere thanks and appreciation.

Care of My Environment

👣 I care for my environment. I clean my space and organize my materials. I'm making a positive difference.

👣 I collect my garbage and recycle as much as possible. I'm making a positive difference.

I clean my home and my neighbourhood. I'm making a positive difference.

👣 I use natural resources like paper, water and electricity responsibly. I'm making a positive difference.

My Local Community

☾ I love and respect people of all ages and nationalities. I'm making a positive difference.

❛ I contribute to a happier world. I'm making a positive difference.

☾ I donate the best of my material possessions to those who need them most. I'm making a positive difference.

At Home

★ I notice what needs to get done at home. I plan my day, organize and begin my tasks. I'm making a positive difference.

★ I help my family and friends I love. I'm making a positive difference.

★ I enjoy reading for information and ideas to transform my world and my environment. I can make a positive difference.

All About Me

I am confident, capable, lovable and optimistic. So... I can make a positive difference!

www.ingramcontent.com/pod-product-compliance
Lightning Source LLC
Chambersburg PA
CBHW061401090426
42743CB00002B/102